UNDERSTAND
HOW TO DRAW DS7

Drawing Detail

Sylvia Frattini

SEARCH PRESS

*Crab apple blossom in HB pencil
and ballpoint pen*

Introduction

Detail has always played a vital part in my painting and drawing. As a young child I was always fascinated by highly decorative and complicated subjects and when I look back to my student days I can see that even then my drawings used to display a wealth of detail.

Most of this early work was in fact executed in pen and ink, and I would use the reverse side of the nib to achieve the finest lines. I still do this, but nowadays most of my drawings are produced with a fine ballpoint pen. I find these comfortable to use; at the same time they give me the necessary control for highly detailed work.

Since I trained as a designer, the balance in my work is particularly important to me. I always spend a considerable amount of time, therefore, sketching and planning before I attempt a final drawing; indeed it is not unusual for me to work for as long as two years on preliminary sketches for paintings. The more one plans, the more successful one's finished work will be.

Drawing in detail is not easy, but like most tasks it becomes easier with perseverance. Most aspiring artists will avoid drawing complicated and intricate subjects until they have developed their drawing skills to some degree. Never be discouraged, though, if you find the work particularly difficult, or if you are unable to obtain the amount of detail that you would like. To succeed and have confidence in your work, you must be patient and persevere with your drawings.

Because I take time to complete my work, it is essential to establish beforehand what I intend to include in my pictures in order to avoid alterations later. A great deal of practice and patience is needed to achieve the degree of detail you will see in my finished drawings. As regards subject matter, I am lucky that I do not usually have to look far afield. Apart from the dry-stone walls (or 'dykes'), which are characteristic of the hill country of the north-west of England in Cumbria

2

where I was brought up, I gathered most of the information for the drawings in this book from my own garden. The sheep and lambs were observed, photographed and sketched from the paddock at the bottom of my garden.

The final stages of my pictures may at first sight appear complicated and difficult to achieve. They might even make you wonder how and where to begin. I find it is essentially a question of taking one step at a time. If you can follow my demonstrations stage by stage, I am sure you will succeed, and find that drawing in detail can prove to be a most rewarding and enjoyable experience.

My aim in this book is to give confidence to an aspiring artist and to dispel any fears he or she may have when dealing with highly intricate subjects. The great lesson that I have learnt is to observe carefully and to study closely the beautiful objects that surround us in our everyday lives. Surely it is through simple lack of observation that so much beauty in our world is missed.

Materials

Pencils: for detailed drawing pencils ranging from 8B (very soft), to 9H, (very hard), and F and HB (medium), are perhaps the most flexible of all media. They are easily carried and, used with a sketchbook or other suitable surface, can also be on hand for quick drawing and sketching. Your subject matter should suggest which grade of pencil to use. An ideal pencil for sketching in detail is the F grade or HB, which strikes a happy medium between the soft and hard grades. You will find, when you are sketching over a long period with a pencil softer than F and HB, that it will require constant sharpening.

Carbon pencils: these are soft and difficult to keep sharp. They smudge easily and therefore a fixative must be used on the drawing.

Charcoal pencils: these are more easily sharpened than carbon pencils and are preferable for detailed drawing. If you use these pencils your drawings must also be fixed to avoid smudging.

Coloured pencils: these are the most versatile of all the pencils; certain well-known brands can act as a substitute for watercolours, as they will produce washes of colour when dipped in water. Pencil crayons used in conjunction with lead pencils produce some interesting effects. There is now a wide range of colours available, but for sketching in detail I recommend using pencils with thin leads.

Pens: two main kinds of drawing pen are the fountain pen and the dip pen; both are ideal for fine work. Mapping pens are a finer version of the dip pen. Whenever I require an extra fine line, I use the back of the nib. Graphic pens are now available in a variety of thicknesses. These provide a quick method of sketching and are easy to handle. Ballpoint pens are my own favourite drawing medium. They are so easy to use and give me all the control I need for very fine work.

Fibre-tipped pens: these are available in a wide variety of shaped tips, but for detailed drawing I use the thin, harder tips.

Drawing papers: these range from smooth to rough. For detailed work choose a smooth paper which easily takes a fine line. Always choose good quality paper as it is so much more pleasant to work on.

Drawing flowers

It is usually simple enough to draw a variety of floral shapes, yet to arrange them together in a complementary way requires hard thought and experience. Once the early technical problems have been mastered, it is important to look not only at the flower shapes, but also at the spaces between them.

Practice drawing flower heads or blossom in varying positions initially to the same size and proportion of the plant. If this proves too difficult, then enlarge the scale of your drawing. Study the flowers closely and carefully and pay particular attention to the inside of the flower.

Stamens form an interesting pattern which makes a delightful contrast to petals. Study how flowers and leaves are attached to the main stem. Extend your drawing further by adding flowers; alternatively, try drawing only the main outline of the plant. Even a simple linear sketch made with ballpoint pen can be attractive.

Throughout most of the year I sketch and paint, on average some thirty hours every week. But from late spring to midsummer I take a break and work in the garden. Besides enjoyment, gardening provides me with the necessary time to plan my work for the year ahead. I particularly like wild flowers, so much so that I am reluctant to remove any from my garden. How many of us stop to look closely at the delicate features of the birds-eye speedwell or the bindweeds, both of which look beautiful in abundance? Nor should we forget the amazing formation of the dandelion clock.

Before attempting a final drawing, I spend a long time sketching, photographing, planning and examining plants I intend to use. When studying plants, I try to understand how they grow – each one has its own special characteristics. Having photographed each plant several times, just in case they die before I am able to draw them, I use no less than fifty photographs in the planning of a detailed picture like 'Summer flowers' I cut out the larger shapes separately in paper and arrange them in a variety of ways to achieve the best results before planning the whole design on tracing paper. Here proportion and correct placing are important aspects to consider. Knowing I am about to spend some considerable time working on the picture, I stretch the paper to provide a permanently flat surface to work on. I do this by immersing the paper in water for a few minutes then laying it onto a clean board. I fix it to the board with brown gum strip and allow any surplus water to run off freely before I leave the board flat to dry out. Any wrinkles in the paper will dry out as it contracts. The whole drawing is completed in outline before any detail is added.

Summer flowers

This demonstration, which is as viewed from above, displays a variety of flowers and insects that enjoy my garden every year. This is an exercise based on the relationship between shapes and spaces and the different patterns and lines make it an absorbing and most rewarding study. Texture also plays an important part in the design. I worked on the drawing during late summer and, with the exception of the huge dragonfly and comma butterfly, was able to sketch entirely from life. There is no real substitute for drawing from nature first-hand. Luckily I was able to photograph the dragonfly and comma butterfly, as they were first-time visitors to my garden the year I drew this picture. The red admiral, painted lady and peacock butterflies are part of a collection I have gathered over the years.

At all times during the execution of 'Summer flowers' I leant on a loose scrap of paper to avoid the risk of damaging or smudging the drawing.

Stage 1
In fine pencil I draw the outlines of the fuchsia flowers, the hydrangea leaves and the butterfly; then I fill in the spaces with the smaller begonia flowers and buds.

Stage 2
Again with pencil, I add detail and texture to all of the shapes, in particular the pattern to the butterfly's wings and the vein structure to the flowers and leaves.

Stage 3
I now begin to shade in varying tones, paying particular attention to those shapes which appear beneath the others. To these I apply the deepest tones.

Stage 4
I block-in the background spaces with a ballpoint pen to create a sense of depth to the whole design.

Stage 5—the finished picture *(see pages 6, 7)*
I continue adding detail, texture and patterns until I feel I have captured the subject in all its rich detail and diversity.

Stage 1

Stage 2

Stage 3

Stage 4

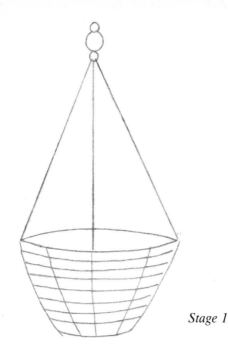

Stage 1

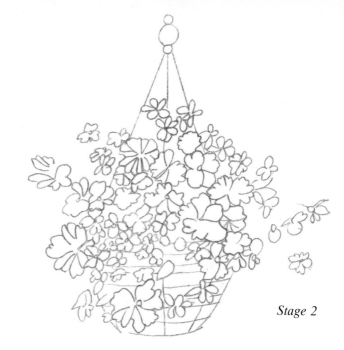

Stage 2

Hanging basket

This hanging basket, with its lovely profusion of flower heads, makes an interesting study.

Stage 1

I draw the main lines of the hanging basket in pencil, but I keep the sketch light as the lines which still show at the final stage may need to be erased.

Stage 2

I continue, in pencil, adding some of the larger nasturtium flowers and leaves, begonias and geraniums to the basket.

Stage 3

Now, using ballpoint pen, I fill in the remaining leaves and flowers, after which I begin to shade some of the larger flowers and block-in parts of the background area.

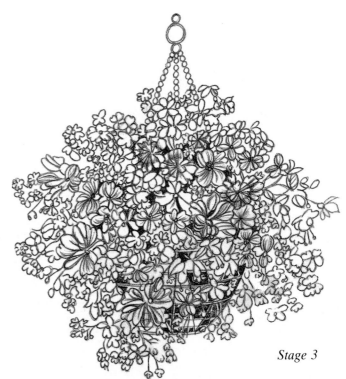

Stage 3

Stage 4—the finished picture

I continue adding detail until I achieve the sense of opulence and abundance that this hanging basket arouses in me.

Stage 4 – the finished picture

A profusion of hanging baskets and summer flowers that provide me with so much pleasure.

10

Drawing blossom

When drawing complicated plants like cherry and apple blossom with their abundance of flowers, most artists will not attempt a final drawing without first closely studying and understanding the subject and sketching several views of it.

Blossom comprises of lovely, delicate flowers which need careful consideration if they are to make as beautiful a drawing. The design as a whole needs variety and balance, and selection is a most important part of the design. Because of its intricate nature, it is necessary to decide whether to include all or several of the flower heads and leaves.

I suggest that you plan the layout of your design, to avoid an imbalance or lean, towards one side of the paper. If you choose a paper of a reasonable size, you can always trim away any waste after the drawing has been completed, whereas it is difficult to add more paper!

Cherry blossom

When drawing blossom I lightly sketch out the main shapes of the flower heads and leaves, using only a ballpoint pen; but because of the delicate nature of the plant I suggest that, if you are a beginner, you sketch very lightly with a pencil, so that the lines can be erased and drawn again and again until the structure of the plant is correct.

Stage 1

After drawing the basic structure of the cherry blossom lightly in pencil, I consider the form and shape of the flower heads and buds, and draw a simple but precise outline of each one. As the nature of this blossom is so delicate, draw the lines fine enough to be erased if necessary.

Stage 1

Stage 2

Continue drawing with equally fine lines using ballpoint pen and add the characteristic details to the flowers and buds. Here I also introduce leaf veins and details of texture on the stalks.

Stage 2

Stage 3—the finished picture

I develop the shadows and the leaf forms, and begin working on the detail in the centre of the flower heads, as well as strengthening the flower stalks. The last element is to finalise the detail in the centre of the flowers. From the centre to the outside of the flowers I work shadows, dark to light, with the darkest shading at the very centre. This, of course, is the area where there is least light. I shade carefully between the stamens, and finally, with a very fine point, I sharpen up the drawing of the stamens themselves.

Stage 3 – the finished picture

1 Autumn leaves in ballpoint pen

Drawing leaves, patterns and textures

We are not always so quick to notice that leaves can be as interesting as flowers to draw, despite flowers' brilliant colours. Have you ever looked closely at dried autumn leaves, with their twisted shapes? If there are no flowers available to draw during the winter, you do not need to look far for a subject.

Leaves with colour patterns, however, present a problem to the artist. The colour patterns on the leaves emphasize the design. There is no real difficulty in adding them to a linear drawing as seen here in sketch 4, but when it is necessary to add shading to your drawing, you will be required to sort out the two quite different pencil tones; these will describe both colour and form and must not be confused. You could emphasize either. In sketch 5, I have chosen to stress the shading more than the colour markings.

The autumn leaves are rendered in ballpoint pen and the cultivated ivy is rendered with a coloured wash and ballpoint pen.

2 Cultivated ivy using a coloured wash
  and ballpoint pen

3 Linear drawing of ivy
  in 2H pencil

4 Variagated pattern in
  2H and HB pencil

5 Variagated pattern and
  shade in 2H, HB
  and ballpoint pen

Honeysuckle in ballpoint pen. The honeysuckle, combined with hedge ivy and ground bindwort, contrasts well with the wren on page 19 to produce a highly detailed and decorative panel.

Drawing birds and animals

Birds and animals are difficult subjects to draw in detail as they are seldom still, yet in order to make ourselves familiar with their character and structure, it is important to be able to sketch from life. If you can get close enough to your subject, try and capture the overall shape and proportions. Study it carefully; watch it move and observe how it stands. Your drawing will be more convincing if you can catch these preliminary impressions correctly before you add other details. Family pets are ideal subjects on which to practice.

I am lucky in having a variety of wild birds in my garden, but to draw them in detail I find it necessary to work from photographs. My camera is always loaded and ready for use for, as with the fledgeling blackbird, (see below), I sometimes need to act quickly. He was the last bird to leave the nest, which had been built fairly close to my back door. I managed to photograph him several times before he dropped out of the nest and disappeared into the surrounding ivy. I then used the remainder of the film to take close-up shots of the nest and ivy.

Wren

This demonstration can be seen on the following two pages. The wren is a frequent visitor to my garden, but as he is so swift in his movements, sadly I only ever catch a fleeting glimpse of him. For this picture, therefore, I had to rely on studies I made of the wren during visits to my local museum. Plants and foliage combine and contrast well with the wren to produce a highly detailed and decorative border panel.

Stage 1

I make numerous sketches to establish the character of the wren and similarly to familiarise myself with the honeysuckle and ivy plants. Carefully, I make a pencil drawing of the central subject and then start to surround it with outlines of the plant forms.

Stage 2

Using ballpoint pen, I now add detail to the honeysuckle leaves and flowers. When drawing the veins on the ivy leaves, I take extra care because, at a later stage, they will remain light in tone while the surrounding area is shaded in.

Stage 3

I block-in the background areas in order to make the bird and plant shapes stand out and then add detail to the drawing of the twigs.

Stage 4

Here I introduce some tonal pencil shading to the plants and flowers, and I begin to shade the ivy leaves while allowing the veins to remain light in tone. I also begin to draw in the detail of the bird's feathers using the ballpoint pen.

Stage 5—the finished picture

I continue to work on the leaves with tonal shading, leaving certain areas of the ivy to suggest its shiny surface. I work as delicately as possible into all the shapes except for the bird. Lastly, and with very fine lines, I add still more detail to the bird's feathers and other areas of the body, working light to dark, and deepen the background where I wish to sharpen its effect.

Stage 1

Stage 2

Stage 3

Stage 4

Stage 5 – the finished picture

Fledgeling blackbird

I spotted this blackbird's nest soon after the eggs were laid. It was quite well hidden within an ivy bush inside a hedge. From the design aspect it seemed an ideal subject to draw, since it offered numerous contrasts in the shapes and textures of the ivy leaves, twigs and straw. I liked the way the ivy made a frame around the nest, and my picture would be completed with the arrival of the little birds.

Having waited so patiently for the right moment to photograph the birds, I almost missed my chance when, on one of my routine checks, I discovered that two of the fledgelings had already flown, leaving only one for me to photograph and draw. I took pictures of this remaining fledgeling from different angles and at varying distances, so that I would not be limited to including only one bird in the final drawing.

Except for the bird, I was able to work outdoors with this picture, and although I did take several photographs of the ivy, I only used them to give me the most interesting aspect of the plant. I already had one nest in my collection, so I was able to leave the nest in the garden undisturbed.

Stage 1

I outline the bird and the leaf shapes lightly in pencil. I suggest the nest by introducing the main twigs and by placing the bird's principal features. I also add a few plant stems, and concentrate the interest towards the centre of the picture.

Stage 2

Next I draw in the variegated patterns on the ivy leaves with ballpoint pen, and increase the detail of the nest formation.

Stage 3

To heighten the veins on the ivy leaves, I introduce some tonal shading with the ballpoint pen. Then I fill in certain of the areas between the leaves, making sure to keep the darkest tones *behind* the bird. This helps to create a feeling of depth in the picture.

Stage 4—the finished picture

I continue to work into all areas of the drawing, particularly the blackbird itself, until I achieve the effect I am after of 'thistledown' softness in the fledgeling's feathers.

Sketches of three feathers in ballpoint pen

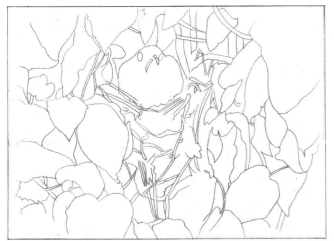

Stage 1

Stage 2

Stage 3

Stage 4 – the finished picture

21

Primroses

Each season has its own special beauty, but I find that, in the spring, the primroses, growing in abundance, not only make a beautiful sight, but provide plenty of interest for the artist. Primroses form part of the background for the hedgehog demonstration described opposite.

Linear sketch in ballpoint pen showing flower formation

Primroses in ballpoint pen.
I have used primroses to form
the background of the demonstration
drawing described opposite.
The finished drawing is shown
on page 25.

Hedgehog in pen and ink.

Hedgehog

In the compost heap in the corner of my garden live a family of hedgehogs. I see them frequently during the summer and autumn evenings, when they venture out looking for food; but on only one occasion in all the years they have occupied the garden have I seen one appear during the daytime.

One spring afternoon I was aware, whilst gardening, of something passing alongside me. Assuming it must be Cora, my pet spaniel, I continued working; however, realising that the dog was not with me, I glanced at the hedge behind me and saw a hedgehog scurrying away.

Knowing this was a rare opportunity, which I could not afford to miss, I walked towards the hedgehog which immediately curled up into a ball. I ran back to the house for my camera and returned just in time to catch the hedgehog unwrapping itself. I took two photographs before he disappeared into the compost heap.

Guessing that at some future time the hedgehog would appear in one of my pictures, I photographed the area where I had seen him. The ivy-clad trees provided an interesting background. I also took photographs of the foreground. Lastly I photographed the wire fence which keeps the sheep out of my garden. The following five stages can be seen on the next two pages.

Stage 1

Having made myself familiar with the hedgehog's characteristics, by sketching him in various positions, I now draw his outline in pencil together with some of the larger leaves and primroses which will form part of the background to the finished picture.

Stage 2

Next I add detail both to the background and the foreground, particularly by drawing in some twigs and dried leaves.

Stage 3

Here I begin to work the spines of the hedgehog with short lines drawn quickly. I add some tonal shading to the leaves, but avoid filling in the veins because I want them to appear light in tone.

Stage 4

Using ballpoint pen, I continue describing the animal's spines by making the short lines define their direction. I begin this very lightly and work into the body several times, on each occasion with an increased depth of line. After this I shade the area surrounding the hedgehog more deeply, again working from light to dark.

Stage 5—the finished picture

I fill in some of the areas between the leaves and flowers in order to give more importance to the plant structures, and I suggest the pattern of the background wire. I work further into the hedgehog's body, taking extra care to highlight the tips of the spines, and continue until I am satisfied with the degree of detail and verisimilitude.

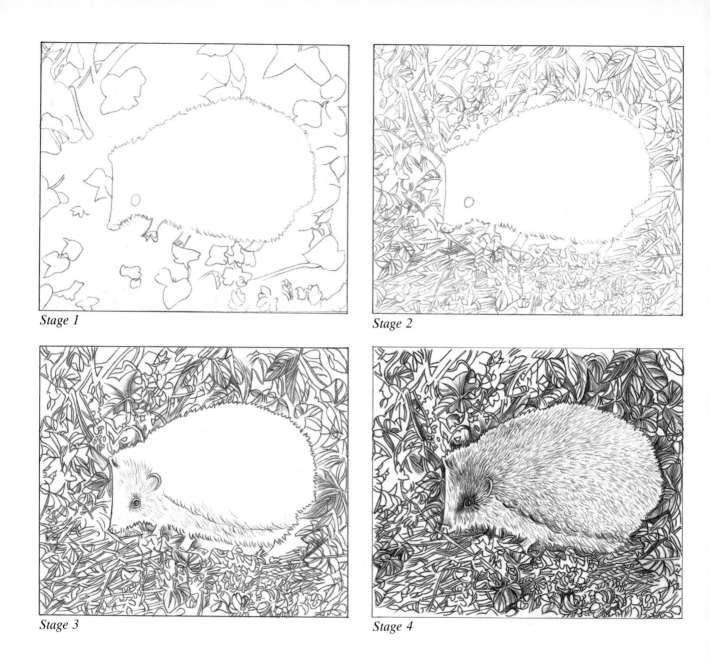

Stage 1

Stage 2

Stage 3

Stage 4

Stage 5 – the finished picture

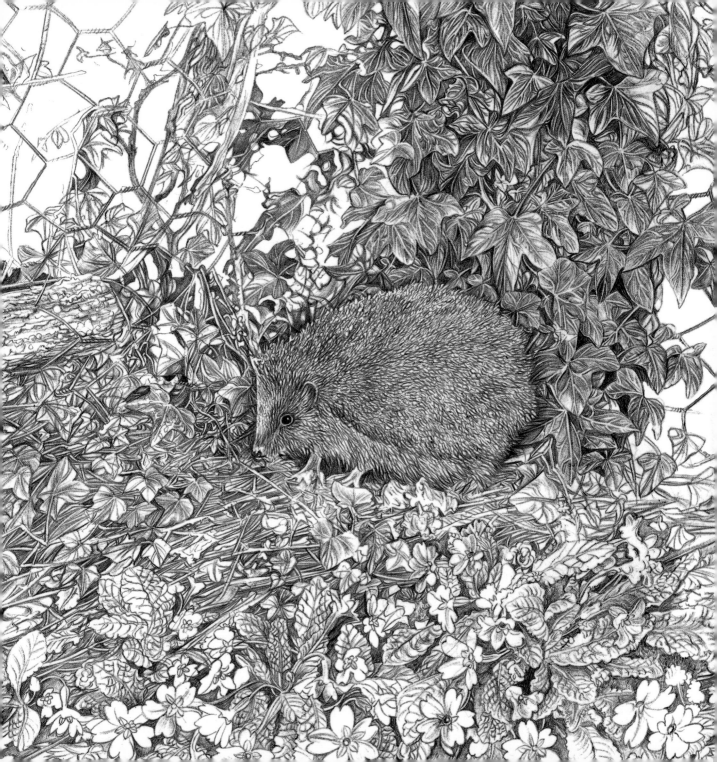

Lambs in ballpoint pen.

Old oak tree and lambs

Some years ago, when travelling through Gloucester-shire to the Forest of Dean, I noticed a group of lambs playing around an old oak tree. On the return journey I stopped to take a closer look at the tree, particularly to investigate the bark formation, with its characteristic irregularities. The exposed root structure not only presented a fascinating and intricate study in itself, but it also offered a striking contrast to the huge vertical mass of the trunk. That gave me an irresistable centrepiece for both a painting and a drawing, but the lambs, unfortunately, had disappeared. However, I photographed the tree both at a distance and close to; and, of course, the closer I came to the tree trunk, the wealthier the bark characteristics were shown to be.

Before starting on the final work, I made repeated sketches from other sources, notably the old trees and roots in the sheepfold at the bottom of my garden.

Stage 1

I make a fine pencil drawing in order to establish the tree trunk, suggesting some of the bark formation and

the root structures. At the same time, I indicate the ground area surrounding the tree.

Stage 2

Continuing with fine pencil lines, I add more of the bark characteristics and extend the groundwork around the roots of the tree.

Stage 3

Using ballpoint I emphasize the basic form by tonal light and shade. This gives strength to the trunk and accentuates its solidity. The shadows are fairly clear with the light source coming from the right-hand side of the picture.

Stage 4

Still using a ballpoint pen, I further strengthen the darker tones, particularly inside the hollows of the tree. These should be quite strong. I continue to work into the complex bark formation, and draw the blades of grass surrounding the tree with greater precision. I also begin to add some leaf detail.

Stage 1

Stage 2

Stage 3

Stage 4

27

Stage 5 – the finished picture

Stage 5—the finished picture

I continue to work into the whole area until the degree of detail I have achieved satisfies me. The old tree in itself provides sufficient interest to make a satisfying picture, perhaps with some distant hills added to complete the scene. Here I have decided, instead, to introduce some very young lambs To achieve the best combined effect, I make several sketches, on tracing paper, of lambs in different groupings. Then I lay each tracing on top of the tree drawing. Once I am happy with the positioning I draw the lambs on to the base picture.

The watchful mother

The picture on page 31 is based on sketches I made up in the Cumbrian hills and on photographs taken during a showery afternoon. For my watercolours, I particularly like to photograph dry-stone walls either during or after the rain, as the colours of the lichens and mosses are then at their best.

Weathered stone walls with their irregular shapes and enormous range of textures set an ideal challenge for me. As I am so interested in detail, I find these walls a rich source of delight to draw.

I have used the stone wall in the demonstration drawing overleaf, together with its equally weathered post, as a focal point in the picture, and have included the sheep and lambs, whose woolly coats provide a detailed contrast. To give a sense of distance to the picture I have set in the background a peaceful fell scene of the sort that frequently appears in my paintings.

Stage 1

First, using pencil, I outline the shapes of the animals against the stone wall behind them and the wooden post. I include the fell scene to the right of the picture.

Stage 2

Next, with a ballpoint pen, I add details of the moss and lichen that cling to the wall, and of the texture of the stones themselves. I try to emphasize in particular the shapes of the stones. I also add detail to the background landscape.

Stage 3

Still using a ballpoint pen and working from light to dark, I now give some tonal shading to the wall and the post. I begin working into the sheep and lambs, and in particular their coats where I try to create a convincing 'woolly' effect. I also introduce the grass.

Stage 4—the finished picture

I continue adding detail to all areas until I have achieved the full degree of liveliness, density and involvement which is implicit in the subject. To me that is the reason for portraying it.

Fell sheep in pen and ink.

Stage 1

Stage 2

Stage 3

Stage 4 – the finished picture

30

31

First published in Great Britain 1989 by Search Press Limited,
Wellwood, North Farm Road, Tunbridge Wells,
Kent TN2 3DR

Text and drawings by Sylvia Frattini

Text, illustrations, arrangement and typography copyright ©
Search Press Limited 1989

U.S. Artists Materials Trade Distributors:
Winsor & Newton, Inc.
11 Constitution Avenue, P.O. Box 1396, Piscataway,
NJ 08855-1396

Canadian Distributors:
Anthes Universal Limited
341 Heart Lake Road South, Brampton, Ontario L6W 3K8

Australian Distributors:
Jasco Pty Limited
937-941 Victoria Road, West Ryde, N.S.W. 2114

New Zealand Distributors:
Caldwell Wholesale Limited
Wellington and Auckland

ISBN 0 85532 611 5

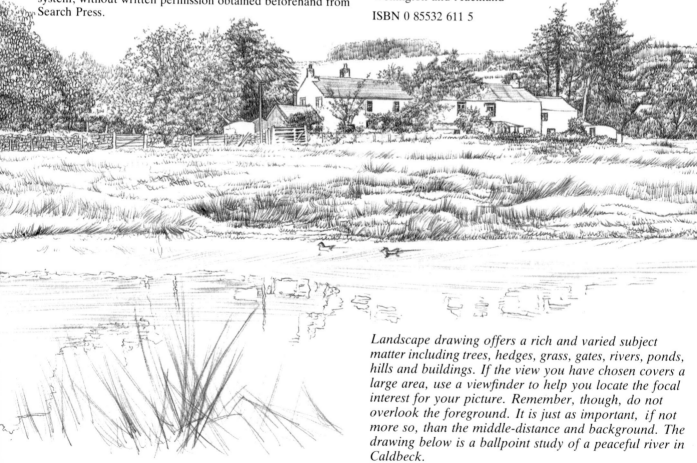

*Landscape drawing offers a rich and varied subject
matter including trees, hedges, grass, gates, rivers, ponds,
hills and buildings. If the view you have chosen covers a
large area, use a viewfinder to help you locate the focal
interest for your picture. Remember, though, do not
overlook the foreground. It is just as important, if not
more so, than the middle-distance and background. The
drawing below is a ballpoint study of a peaceful river in
Caldbeck.*

Typeset by Scribe Design, 123 Watling Street, Gillingham, Kent. Made and printed in Spain by A.G. Elkar S. Coop. Bilbao-12